T0198816

The Golden Threads Of My Life

ANNETTE BUCHANAN-PHILLIPS

Copyright © 2021 by Annette Buchanan-Phillips. 823726

All rights reserved. No part of this book may be reproduced or
transmitted in any form or by any means, electronic or mechanical,
including photocopying, recording, or by any information storage
and retrieval system, without permission in writing from the
copyright owner.

To order additional copies of this book, contact:
Xlibris
844-714-8691
www.Xlibris.com
Orders@Xlibris.com

ISBN: Softcover   978-1-6641-5576-3
         EBook   978-1-6641-5575-6

Print information available on the last page

Rev. date: 01/30/2021

Dedication:

"Those with pure love do all they can to let their mates grow in every way. Detached love means to let others exist without forcing our will upon them. That is spiritual love."

-Harold Klemp

"The Language of Soul"

All art and text by Annette Buchanan- Phillips

Contents

Index of Plates

All art and photography are the creations of
Annette Buchanan-Phillips
no reprints without permission.

#1
For all we know,
There may never be
another opportunity to
say what was in our
hearts,
that day.
The last time, the time
never before,
never again.
Love will never know an end.
Maybe in love terrible things
will go away.
A.B.P '93

#2
God called
in a dream...
We speak of it...
Act on desire to fulfill the
prophecy-
Form; then manifest
the reality...
And bring forth that
we created
Fruit;
and proof of our alliance
with God.
A.B.P. '93

#3
Little boy blue
born alone-
no mother to hold you,
no father, no home
the world has no
place for you
God is the way
for you to be free
at last, Love is
the path to take
to your brighter
day.
A.B.P. '89

10

To You

You kissed me
and joy
crept into my senses
penetrated through
rock solid defenses
a rectifying,
sanctifying
baptismal bliss
caressed my soul.

A.B.P.

Conquered

This starvation
is the diet
that you
put me on because
I was human enough
to fall-
and woman enough to know
when I am
conquered. I beg of
you
mercy. Love me again.
A.B.P.

Secret

Delicious secret
unlike any other
I will rankle,
beg and bother
to keep you...
All mine.

A.B.P.

Open minds,
Open hearts,
Open arms,

InterAct Cleveland.

Unification

I am the bridge from earth to heaven,
I am the wire through which God flows,
When He passes through me I am a magnet,
Attracting with Love wherever I go.
Love from Heaven, meets Love from earth;
The kingdom of heaven is returned to the earth.
Praise ye the Lord on High;
Praise Him within;
Praise Love for all you're worth
By Love give Him.
As it shines in heaven;
Love shine on the earth;
Live Love in Heaven;
Live Love on earth.
I am the channel from earth to glory;
out from my belly living water flows;
Thy will is done on earth; as is in heaven;
Thy kingdom extended from heaven below.
A.B.P.

Time

Should there ever come a
day when I no longer
come to bear
upon your thoughts
then pause
and realize
that being never comes
to naught-
The good, the bad within
us, strive till one
becomes the victor
the Spirit is the prize...
Eternity at last.

A.B.P.

If

If there had been time
we might have walked
along the beach
sand and waves singing
love songs
silent to be felt
much more than heard
like the flutter of
hearts more than of wings
what loving might have
liberated
remains the question more than
the answer
when thinking more than speaking
"might have been."
A.B.P

Belief

Belief in me has never been
required-
Believe instead in God
who cannot fail:
Obedience to me never was
a requisite-
Obey God who will deliver
and is unable to be in error
Loving me was not
prerequisite to receive
my love-
Love God who does
provide all life alone.
A.B.P

Ascension

My love for you ascends,
transcends higher than
Jonathan could fly
determined bird,
or vapor rises toward
a drying sun;
Am I insane to hide from
other men-
my fear of them grown greater
day by day:
Or have I returned to as I was,
a babe-
screaming at the sound of their voices
Did I ever change?
And if you were here,
day by day;
Would I fear you too?
A.B.P

Untitled

I have learned to live without food,
nor shelter;
husband, children, sex, job, security, family
everything but God.
Because without God I cannot live.
Therefore I am one with Him
and all mankind
with joy, waiting upon Him,
Serving Him, loving Him
Holding Him within and
without me.
A.B.P.

22

Loneliness

Loneliness killed the bird,
though we enjoyed
his singing for but a moment.
He caused us laughter
and I know our love
stayed with him
when he flew
beyond the veil and left the bars
and cages of this life-
I grieve his empty
space
within my life-
but celebrate his freedom.
Λ.B.P

Anonymously

You don't know me
But somehow, someway,
before-
we were lovers,
maybe more
and now in this time
of life
my heart is open
to your place
inside.
A.B.P

Needlessness

No need to speak
of no harm done.
For loving does reward itself afresh,
at every opportunity;
and lacking of embrace-
it lingers on the
fragrance of memory.
A.B.P

Magnetic

With Love have I
drawn him
magnetic are we,
negative; positive
opposedly...
Timeless, and ageless,
power and flame
Love bring us together
again and again.
A.B.P.

Marriage

What is death,
but time stood still;
When deep within your eyes
no world exists-
just you and I;
I walk inside-
I live;
I die with your every
breath.
My will and yours entwine;
my soul and yours
combine,
and we are whole
one body; one soul.
A.B.P.

Your Voice

I long to hear your voice
tonight,
I want to feel your touch
I'm looking for you
everywhere;
I'm seeing you in everyone;
Love, or madness maybe
That God himself imposed.
Me in you-
you in me...Eternity.
A.B.P.

Clinging

I wasn't the kind
you could depend on to cling
whatever you want to do
whoever you want to see; it's
all okay by me
And yet there's still the
feeling,
the one I can't deny
the one that only you can
conjure up
from my very deep
call it what you want to
the one and only love thing.
A.B.P.

One Woman

One woman cried,
one woman danced,
one woman sat silently
contemplating her existence.
One woman energized,
active-ized,
She fought for something
and one woman gave a hug
and quietly tied her apron.
One woman prayed and
one woman listened
and one woman sat up
realizing
we really are
One woman.
A.B.P.

This Man

How shall I speak
of this gentle
Man above a
whisper-
lest the feeling
disappear,
vanish
in the instant
that I
relish,
the second
that I cherish
can this be real?
All I ever needed,
and most of
what I wanted,
just don't say it-
I really hope to keep it.
I wish silently
however,
love would stay
forever...
A.B.P. (1st impression of Brad)

The New Library

It took three years
but now it stands
a monument to
knowledge-
it holds the lamp
and spans the
breach
between past
and future;
letting in the light
colors invite
people in
to browse
and borrow
from its
stacks.
Wisdom.
A.B.P.

Miracle

"A miracle-"
exclaimed the crowd
and cried-
tears running down
at the sight
of the Shroud
of Turin
rescued
from the Cathedral
in flames
against the midnight
Italian sky.
The burial cloth of
Jesus
emerged
unscathed.
They prayed the precious relic: "saved."
A.B.P. '96

GODDESSES, WHORES, WIVES, AND SLAVES

Women in Classical Antiquity

STRAWBERRY

victories

Bride

BRUTAL TRUTH
WHEN I READ the article,
...rember 1994]...it was not a
Most women ..."Black and
battered women tend to
...un-t to

GRAND

...hand through the key hole, and my
bowels were moved at his touch. 5. I
arose up to open to my beloved. my
hands dropped with myrrh, and my
fingers were full of the choicest
myrrh. 6. I opened the bolt of my
door to my beloved, but he had
turned aside, and was gone. My sou...
...melted when he spoke. I so...

$15,000 it's an ingenious
...to the $39,000 luxury

shame

NAUGHTY

NICE

competitors,

SPOIL

sister

The best are free...

Dazedly she

The Problem

That's the problem
you think you see right
through them,
who do you think you are;
from that kicked chair
you mutter I sit here until
I move elsewhere
and move yourself and your spirit
out from there.
That was what you wanted;
to have me no where.
Alas, I exist-
much to your dismay I'm sure
I exist away from you,
ironic isn't it
that with the door propped open
there was no space for breath
and fresh air in the place;
perhaps you thought you'd find
a place of testimony
against you here. This must be it
the dust, the dirt, you got to
keep.
A.B.P.   '97

Wednesday

We'll sip our tea for two
do what we want,
laugh or cry-
feel what we want
never ask why...
Its our time-
yours and mine;
loving every moment of
Wednesday.
He was married,
I didn't complain-
he only spoke softly when he said my name
Wednesday.
Gentle eyes, quiet smile
he came to play with me for a while
Wednesday.
A.B.P.

No Tomorrow

There is no tomorrow
everyday is yesterday
dark and brooding, malicious as the other
beyond the reason
and words, words go rushing past
the listener
and swirling words,
words go down
the drain of
time
unheard by anything.
Now I've said and written
all the proof-
and painted what can't be accepted
see how crazed
I have become. The proof.
So stand aloof
observe from there
beyond the point
of interest in this one.
A.B.P. Aka "afterthought" '95

My Path

You crossed my path
and on my lifeline
you must be the nearly
invisible crease,
I went under the knife and
they cut out
the part that was you from my heart;
without bitterness-
but with anesthesia...
I didn't feel a thing;
nut your phantom organ still exists
in the place where
you should have been-
you hurt too much,
you had to go.
Surgery is such a painful,
but necessary thing; when parts cease
to function. Somehow I think I
mourn the loss of something I took for
granted
would always be there; and everything is
different, but still the same
somehow.
A.B.P. '96

44

On seeing "RENT" (the movie)

Living on the edge between life and death
Ultimately, we're all alone;
and when it's all over
as you lay in the grave, the angels
will ask you,
"Who did you choose to love?"
Will you say
someone, anyone, everyone?
Maybe you should just
admit that you feared
to connect-
that you will never understand
what you fear;
honestly, what you hate is
your unfortunate disconnection from
the current of Love.
A.B.P. 01/01/07

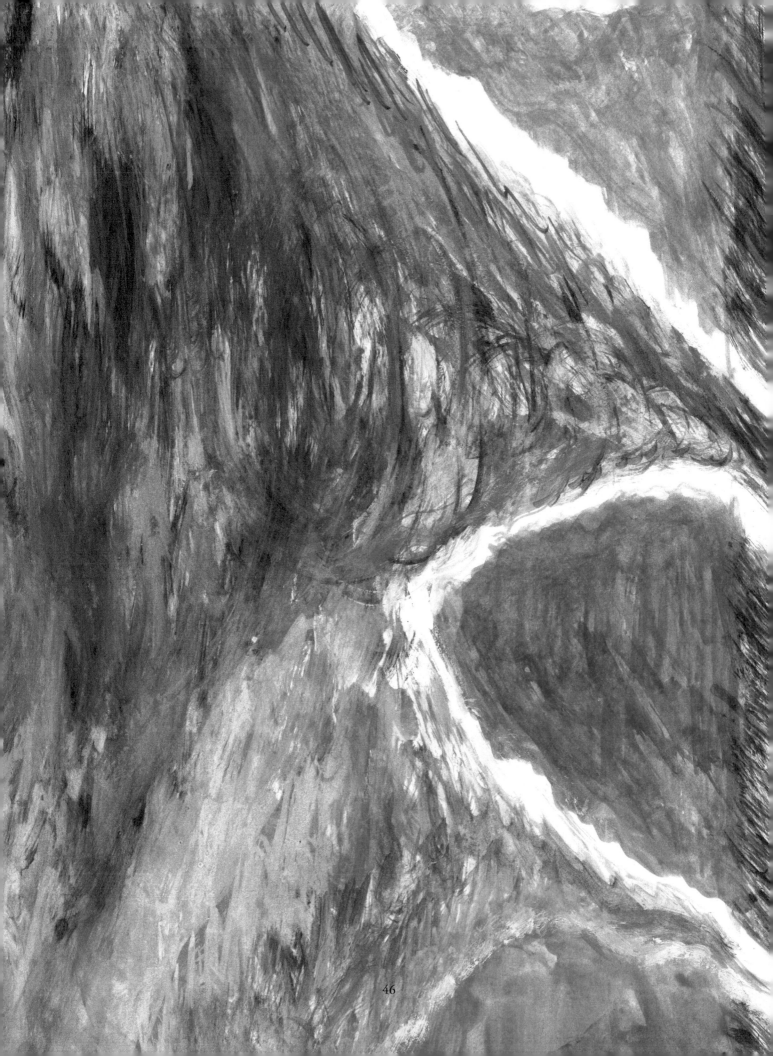

Noisy Mind

He had a noisy mind
which kept
getting in the way
of what I wanted to say
So I chose the silent
communication
of what I did–
but what I did not do
spoke volumes.
A.B.P.

Disappointment

It wasn't love again.
This time no different from
the others,
his schemes-
my dreams,
didn't quite come together
to spell some happy ever after;
and cynicism is all that grows
with every loss of love
to tend it.
This love, I do not recommend it
for the truthful or sincere.
No, not for them.
This love.
A.B.P.

Obsessed

Tall and handsome
wanted
what I could not give;
and he could have been my religion
I could have worshiped
never mind the consequences,
but now it's over...
And the object of my adoration
finds a place
in the realm of all the things
I've loved and lost
in a lifetime.
He was loved when he left,
never to return-
cause of one thing I can't give...
Someone else.
A.B.P. '96

Ballad

Five years without you
I'm not the same,
could have been one day
when you called my name.
Can you disturb the peace?
Can you stoke the fire?
What makes you think
you'd rekindle desire?
I cried when you left,
yes, I suffered-
no explanation;
no excuses offered.
Now you expect
to cause the old sensation
I have to say
love is on vacation.
A.B.P.

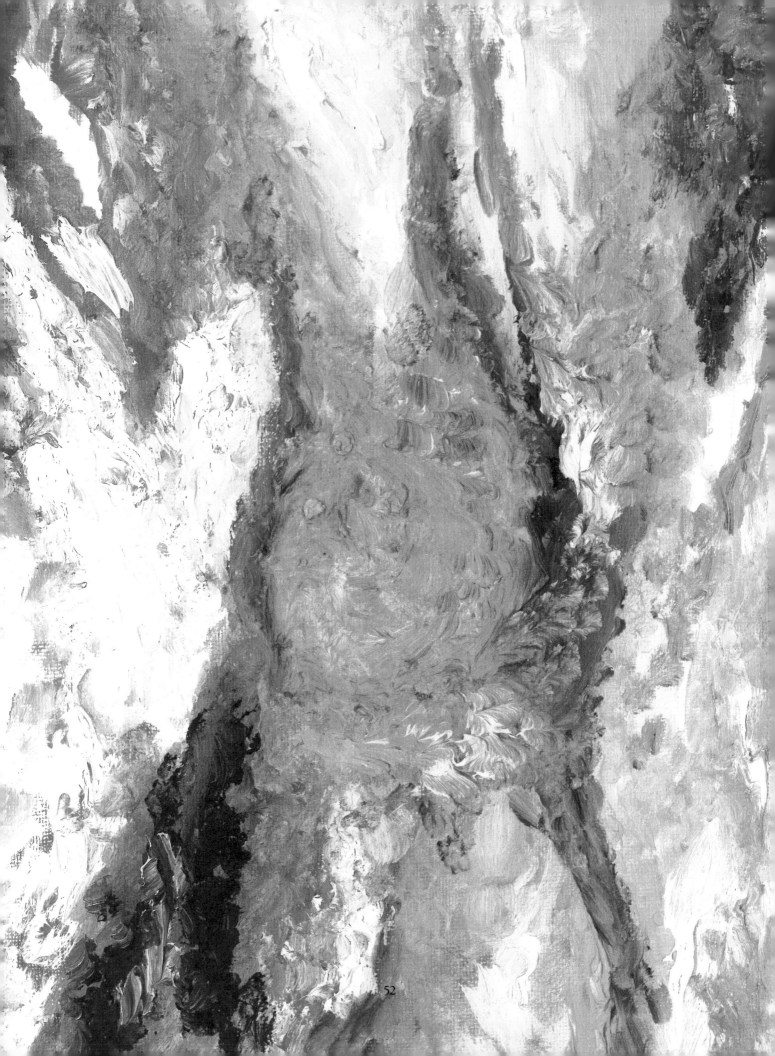

Golden Threads of Life

I see me
present,
future
past-
and love given
gleams brighter
than it's reflection:
love received
but both
were in the loom
as golden threads run through
the fabric of my life.
A.B.P.

Waiting

Waiting
waiting
waiting,
I sit
unable to deny
for all my want
my actions still
belie
the words
I'm not
hoping,
hoping
hoping
for that day
when at last my working
has not
come
to naught.
A.B.P.

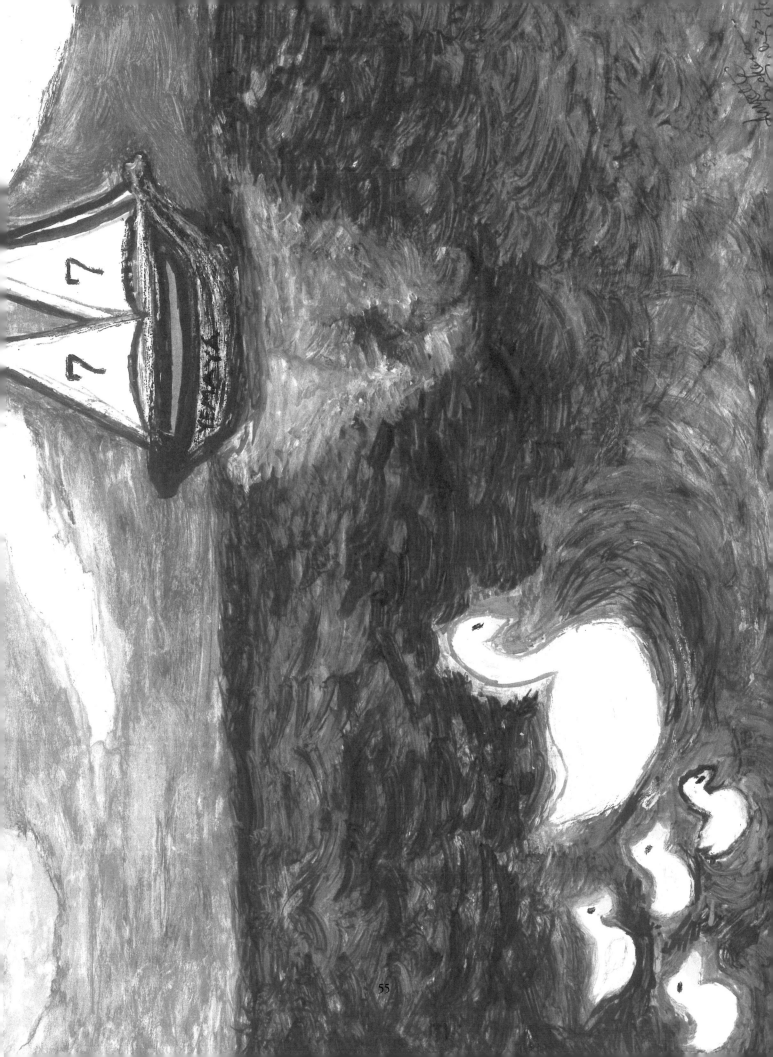

55

After-word

It is finished,
and
my bare soul
between
these pages
lies;
gently judge
for all
of its emotion
is but
only fragments
of me.
A.B.P.

Printed in the United States
By Bookmasters